The Three Little Pigs

Buy the White House

by Dan Piraro

THOMAS DUNNE BOOKS NEW YORK

ST. MARTIN'S GRIFFIN

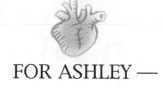

FOR ASHLEY —

the most altruistic person
I have ever known

THOMAS DUNNE BOOKS.
An imprint of St. Martin's Press.

www.stmartins.com

Book design by Dan Piraro

ISBN 0-312-33074-X

10 9 8 7 6 5 4 3

This little piggy worked for Nixon.

This little piggy did too.

This little piggy made millions off of big oil.

his one is a millionaire, too.

And after getting into good schools in spite of his low scores, getting out of going to Vietnam, getting excused when he was AWOL from his National Guard unit, and getting off when he was arrested for DUI, this little piggy's daddy gave him a bunch of businesses that lost millions, gave him a Major League baseball team, got him elected governor of a state where he executed more people than anyone in U.S. history, and got him appointed president of the most powerful country on earth. And he went, "WEE, WEE, WEE" all the way to the White House.

Once in Washington, the Three Little Pigs were in charge of a big, strong country with a foundation made of bricks.

The first thing they did was to begin giving bricks away to their richest friends and replacing them with mud. In this way, they and their friends grew even richer.

But one day, Ari the Weasel
burst in all a-twitter!

"Danger! Danger!" he squealed.
"Lots of people think you bought your way
into the White House and you don't really belong here!
And they think your giving away bricks is making the country weaker!"

"Whatever shall we do?"
cried Dubya.

"Let's send them all three hundred dollars that they were going to get anyway," said Dickey. "That should shut them up."

"Is that what I should tell them?" queried Dubya.

"OF COURSE NOT!" commanded Dickey.

"Tell them these bricks are much too heavy! A lighter country will be stronger!"

And Dubya did what he was told.

Sure enough, $300 was enough to placate the country for a while longer, so the Three Little Pigs were safe again and went back to giving away bricks.

But one day, Ari the Weasel burst in all a-twitter.

"Danger! Danger!" he squealed. "The Big Bad Wolf huffed and puffed and blew a couple of very big buildings down! Everyone is very sad and very frightened and very angry! They're demanding we do something!"

So the Three Little Pigs leapt into action.

"Whatever shall we do?" cried Dubya.

"Announce another tax cut!" shouted Dickey.

"Not yet! For now let's pretend we know where the Big Bad Wolf's hideout is and bomb the crap out of it!" declared Rummy. "And in the meantime, we'll lock up people who LOOK like him!"

"Is that what I should tell them?" queried Dubya.

"NO!" barked Dickey. "Tell them we're going to hunt down the Big Bad Wolf and punish him!"

The country seemed satisfied with this for a while so the Three Little Pigs went back to giving the country's bricks to their rich friends and replacing them with mud.

They were almost completely
finished when, once again, Ari the
Weasel burst in all a-twitter!

"Danger! Danger!" he squealed. "People are upset because we haven't caught the Big Bad Wolf! We need to do something quick!"

"Whatever shall we do?" cried Dubya.

"Let's replace the mud with straw!" declared Dickey.

"And let's go after another Big Bad Wolf. One that will be easier to catch!" shouted Rummy.

"Is that what I should tell them?" Dubya queried.

screamed Dickey and Rummy.

"Tell them the NEW Big Bad Wolf is a friend of the OLD Big Bad Wolf," Rummy advised. "And tell them THIS Big Bad Wolf has Winds of Mass Destruction that he's planning to use to huff and puff and blow our whole country down!"

"And don't mention anything about the straw," oinked Dickey.

And Dubya did what he was told.

So Dubya sent the very same army he went AWOL from so many years before to go get the NEW Big Bad Wolf and his Winds of Mass Destruction. The country seemed satisfied with this for a while, so the Three Little Pigs could start replacing the mud with straw.

And the soldiers didn't even seem to mind that Dubya had gone AWOL before. Instead, they pretended he was a big, brave hero. They even let him play pilot.

But one day, Ari the Weasel burst in again, even more hysterical than before.

"Danger! Danger!" he squealed. "The army has looked everywhere and can't find the NEW Big Bad Wolf or any evidence of his WMD! Our soldiers are dying and people are getting even more angry than before!"

"Whatever shall we do?"
cried Dubya.

"Let's find an even EASIER Big Bad Wolf to catch!" shrieked
Rummy as he clawed at a map of the Middle East.

"Wait!"

declared Dickey, taking a breath and calming everyone down.

Dickey

"Instead, let's give MORE bricks to our friends and a little
of the mud we're replacing with straw to the REGULAR people
in the country. We'll call it a 'middle-class tax cut.' We can
make it back later by using a cheaper grade of straw."

"Is that what I should tell them?" queried Dubya.

Dickey, Rummy and Ari the Weasel just rolled their eyes and sighed.

So Dubya did what he was told. But this time it didn't work as well. People began asking questions. Lots of questions. Questions that Dubya didn't want to answer.

Why aren't we still looking for the FIRST Big Bad Wolf?

Why are we building the country out of straw?

What if ANOTHER Big Bad Wolf decides to huff and puff and blow our country down?

What if that one from Little Red Riding Hood sneaks into the country dressed like a grandma?

Of course, the Three Little Pigs didn't have good answers for any of these questions —

not ones that they cared to share, anyway.

They knew that the people were right; there would always be plenty of Big Bad Wolves and you could never hope to catch them all. And the world is getting smaller everyday.

And a country made of straw isn't a very
good place to hide should a WMD come along.

But the Three Little Pigs didn't care about any of that.

They and their small group of friends had had plenty of time to build their own houses out of highly fortified bricks and surround them with huge moats filled with cash.

And from inside a fortress like that, a Wind of Mass Destruction, no matter how strong, feels like little more than a slight breeze coming off the pool.

t least that's what they were hoping.

But then one day . . .

Ari's replacement, Scott the Armadillo,

burst in all a-twitter...

As a vegan and an animal rights activist, I feel I should vindicate my
innocent nonhuman animal friends. Pigs are not greedy, wolves are not
unnecessarily aggressive and in the real world, presently being run by the most
dangerous and inhumane animals on earth, humans, both of these species
suffer greatly and unjustly. For more information about what you can do to
help the plight of these exploited innocents and their environs, go to
www.farmsanctuary.org and www.defenders.org. And, of course,
vote against Republicans whenever and wherever you can.

ABOUT THE AUTHOR

Dan Piraro is the creator of the syndicated newspaper cartoon, BIZARRO,
which has won three consecutive Reuben Awards from the National Cartoonists Society
for Best Cartoon Panel of the Year. In 2003, Piraro was nominated for its highest award,
Outstanding Cartoonist of the Year.
Dan also tours the country with his one-man stage show, The Bizarro Baloney Show,
a two-hour extravaganza of songs, puppets, art, music, cartoons, costumes, verbs and nouns.
To see more of his work, please visit his Web site at www.bizarro.com.